AF338131

100 FIRST WORDS

French Edition
Reading 3rd Grade

Children's Reading & Writing Books

Hi Kids!

Do you want to know how to speak french?

Let's read and learn common french words.

English	French
I	**je**
of	**de**
is	**est**
not	**pas**

English
the
le
French

English
you
vous
French

English
the
la
French

English
with
avec
French

English
that

que
French

English
a

un
French

English
it

il
French

English
and

et
French

English

will

va

French

English

has

a

French

English

only

ne

French

English

the

les

French

English
this

ce
French

English
in

en
French

English
on

on
French

English
that

ça
French

English
one

une
French

English
have

avoir
French

English
of

pour
French

English
me

moi
French

English
which
qui
French

English
we
nous
French

English
there
y
French

English
but
mais
French

English
in

dans
French

English
well

bien
French

English
she

elle
French

English
while

tout
French

English
more
plus
French

English
my
mon
French

English
about
sur
French

English
what
quoi
French

English
where

où
French

English
good

bon
French

English
same

même
French

English
never

jamais
French

English
watch
voir
French

English
yes/no
Oui/Non
French

English
one
un
French

English
two
deux
French

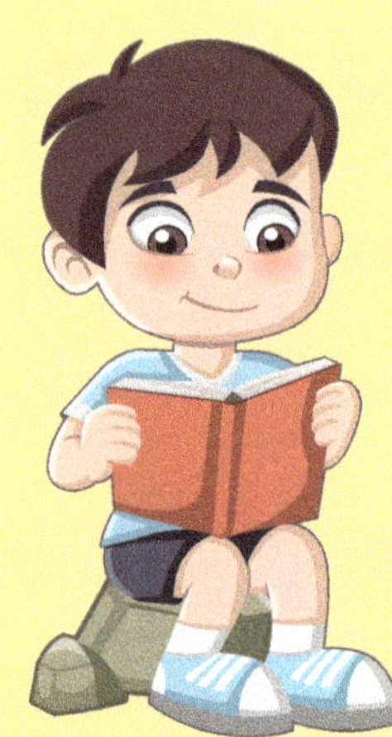

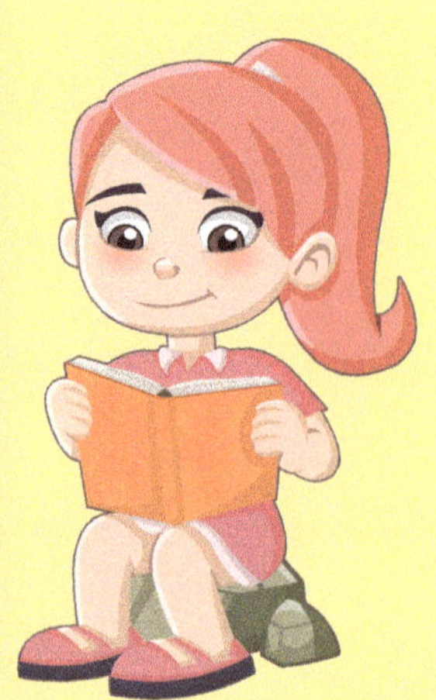

English
three

trois
French

English
four

quatre
French

English
five

cinq
French

English
six

six
French

English
seven

sept
French

English
eight

huit
French

English
nine

neuf
French

English
ten

dix
French

English
Monday
lundi
French

English
Tuesday
mardi
French

English
Wednesday
mercredi
French

English
Thursday
jeudi
French

English
Friday
vendredi
French

English
Saturday
samedi
French

English
Sunday
dimanche
French

English
today
aujourd'hui
French

English
tomorrow

demain
French

English
yesterday

hier
French

English
breakfast

le petit déjeuner
French

English
lunch

le déjeuner
French

English
dinner
le dîner
French

English
food
la nourriture
French

English
chocolate
le chocolat
French

English
sweets
les bonbons
French

English **must**

French **faut**

English **summer**

French **été**

English **can**

French **peut**

English **little**

French **peu**

English

really

vraiment

French

English

time

temps

French

English

always

toujours

French

English

life

vie

French

English
world

monde French

English
go

aller French

English
man

homme French

English
father

père French

English

before

avant

French

English

need

besoin

French

English

wife

femme

French

English

love

aime

French

English
wrong

mal
French

English
speak

parler
French

English
your

vos
French

English
after

après
French

English

small

petit

French

English

mother

mère

French

English

girl

fille

French

English

people

gens

French

LET'S MATCH THE WORDS!

MATCHING EXERCISE

Draw a line to match the English word to its French word.

English		French
with	• •	et
and	• •	monde
me	• •	bon
good	• •	avec
yesterday	• •	moi
world	• •	bonjour
hello	• •	argent
money	• •	hier

Here are some of the french words used in a sentence or phrase.

Fill in the blank with the correct French word.

English	
week	seven days a week

French	
semaine	sept jours par _______________

English	
year	next year

French	
année	_______________ prochaine

Fill in the blank with the correct French word.

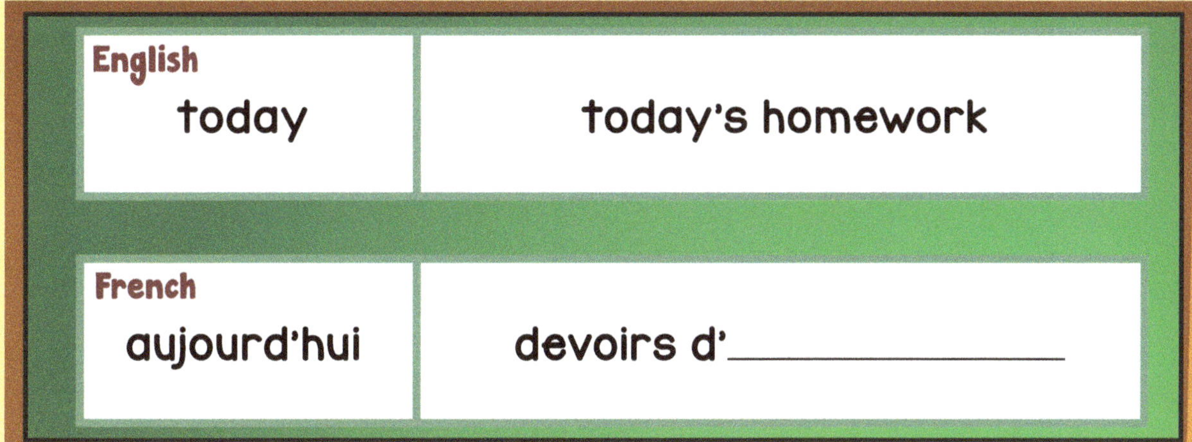

English	
today	today's homework

French	
aujourd'hui	devoirs d'_________________

English	
tomorrow	return tomorrow

French	
demain	revenir _____________

Fill in the blank with the correct French word.

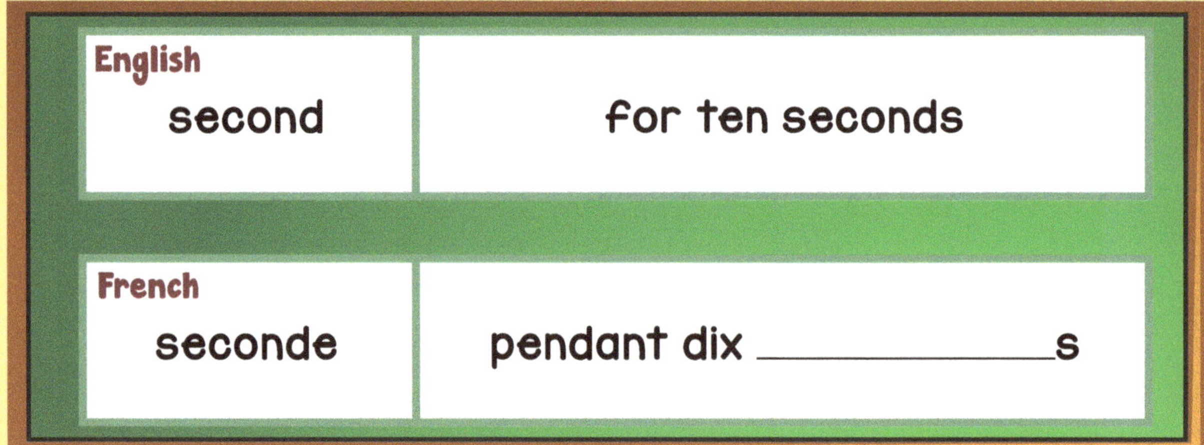

Fill in the blank with the correct French word.

English	
minute	one minute

French	
minute	une ______________

English	
use	use that computer

French	
utiliser	______________ cet ordinateur

Fill in the blank with the correct French word.

English	
do	to do it all

French	
faire	tout _____________

English	
go	go to the store

French	
aller	_____________ au magasin

Fill in the blank with the correct French word.

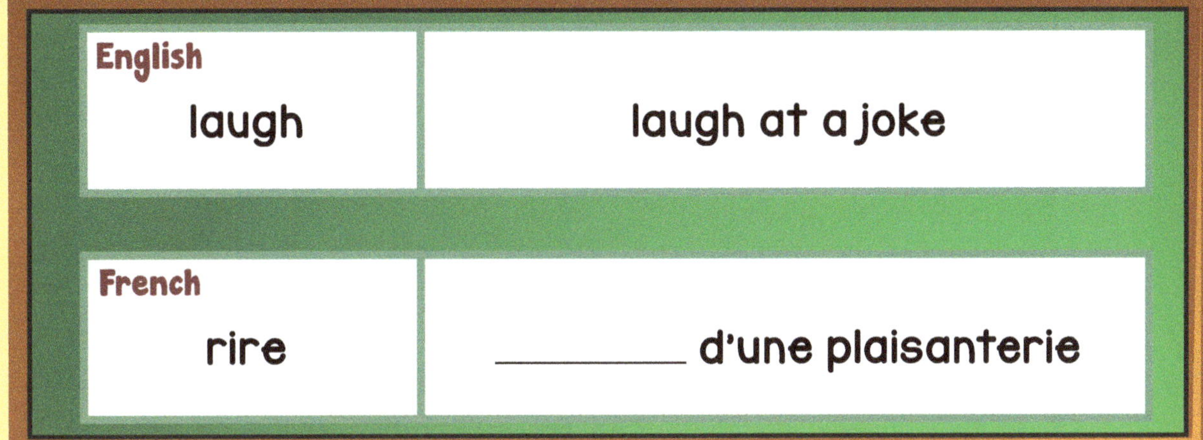

English	
laugh	laugh at a joke

French	
rire	__________ d'une plaisanterie

English	
see	see a sunset

French	
voir	__________ un coucher de soleil

Fill in the blank with the correct French word.

Fill in the blank with the correct French word.

English	
beautiful	very beautiful

French	
belle	très ___________

English	
difficult	very difficult

French	
difficile	très ___________

Fill in the blank with the correct French word.

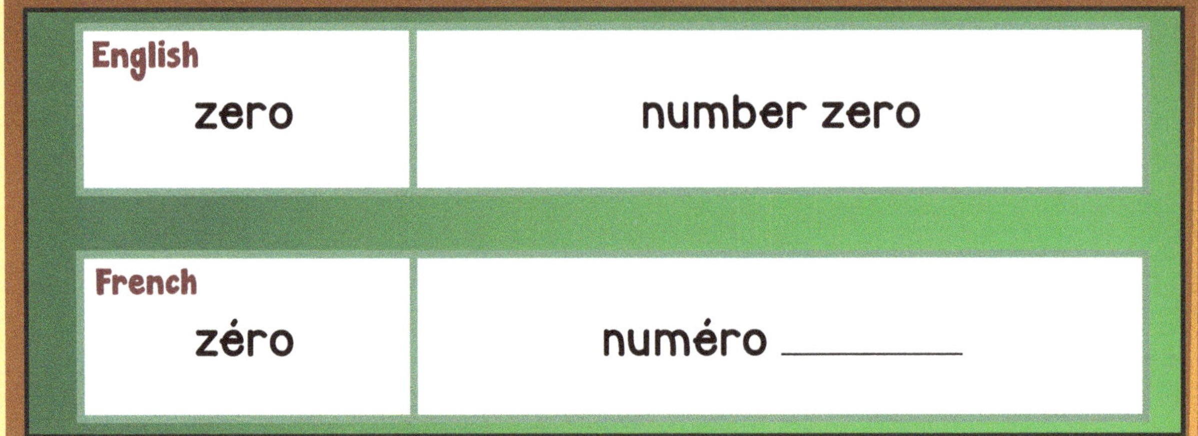

English	
zero	number zero

French	
zéro	numéro _________

English	
one	One of that, please.

French	
un	_______ de ceux-là, s'il vous plaît.

Fill in the blank with the correct French word.

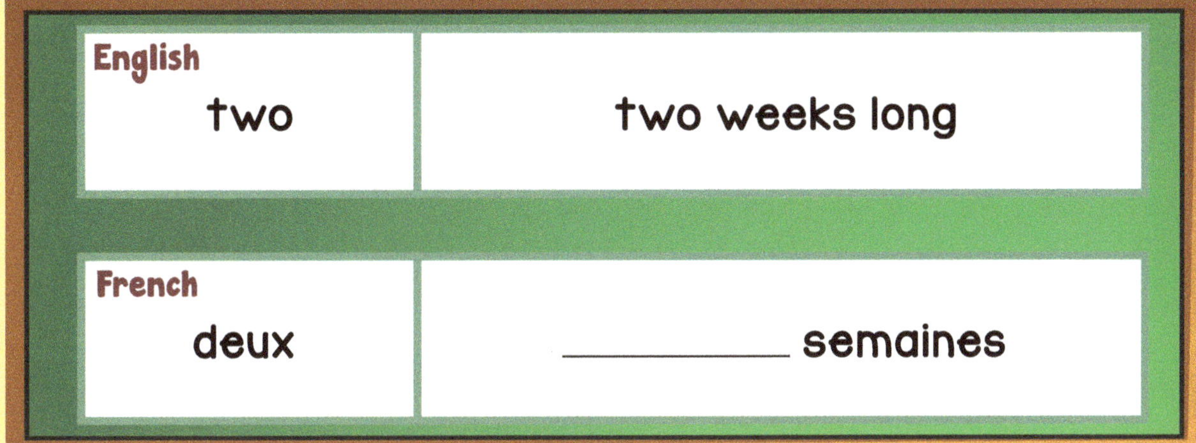

English	
two	two weeks long

French	
deux	__________ semaines

English	
three	number three

French	
trois	numéro __________

Fill in the blank with the correct French word.

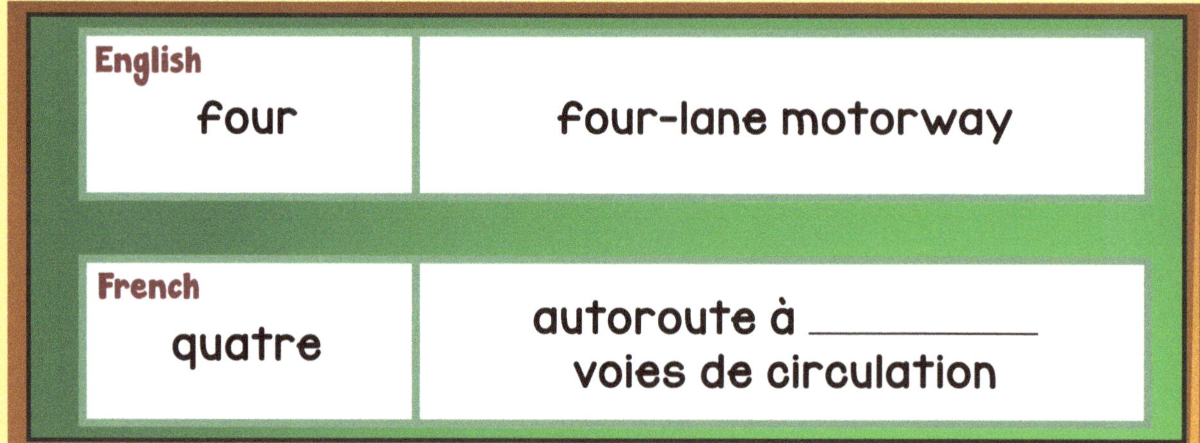

English	
four	four-lane motorway

French	
quatre	autoroute à __________ voies de circulation

English	
five	five degrees

French	
cinq	__________ degrés

Fill in the blank with the correct French word.

English
six
six things
French
six
__________ choses

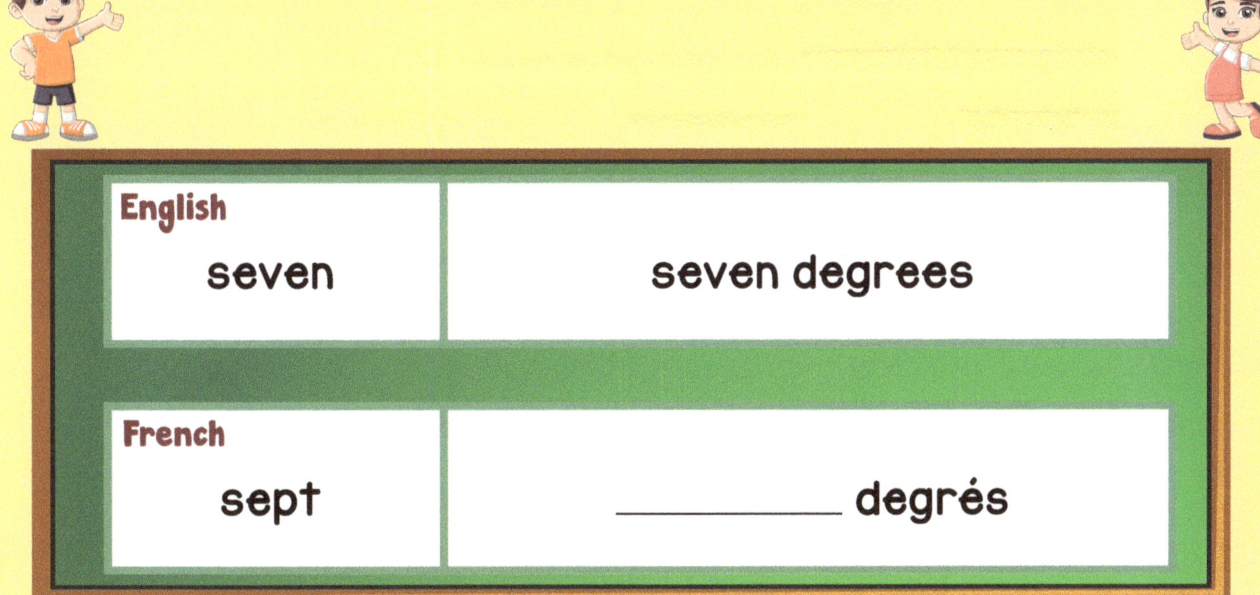
English
seven
seven degrees
French
sept
__________ degrés

Fill in the blank with the correct French word.

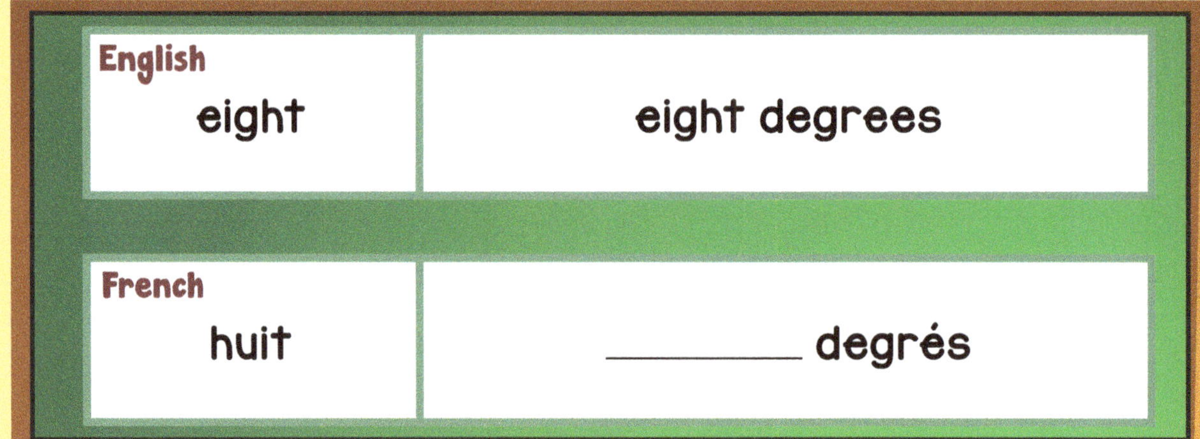

English	
eight	eight degrees

French	
huit	__________ degrés

English	
nine	nine degrees

French	
neuf	__________ degrés

Fill in the blank with the correct French word.

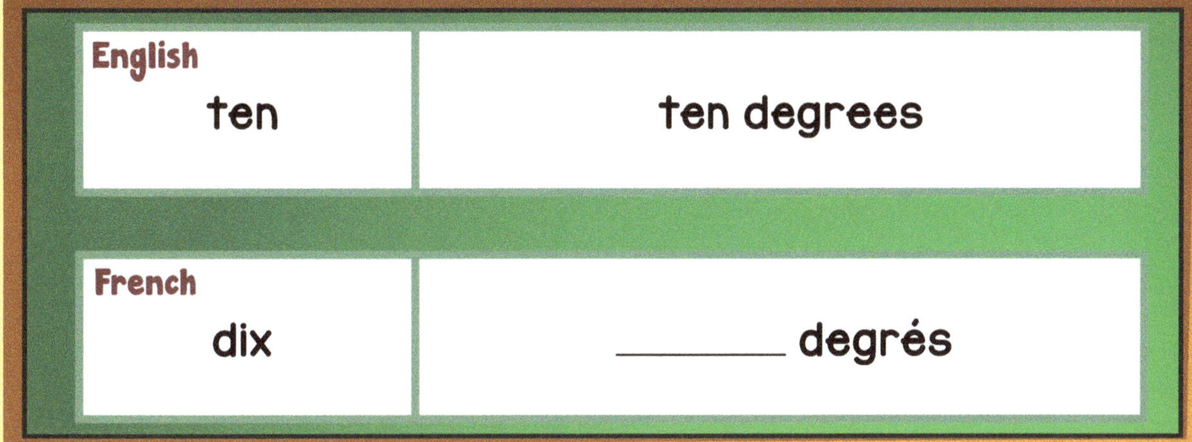

English	
ten	ten degrees

French	
dix	_________ degrés

English	
coffee	cup of coffee

French	
café	tasse de _________

Fill in the blank with the correct French word.

English	
water	drink water

French	
eau	__________ potable

English	
beef	beef steak

French	
boeuf	steak de __________

Fill in the blank with the correct French word.

English	
pork	pork chops

French	
porc	côtelettes de __________

English	
chicken	brown chicken

French	
poulet	__________ marron

Fill in the blank with the correct French word.

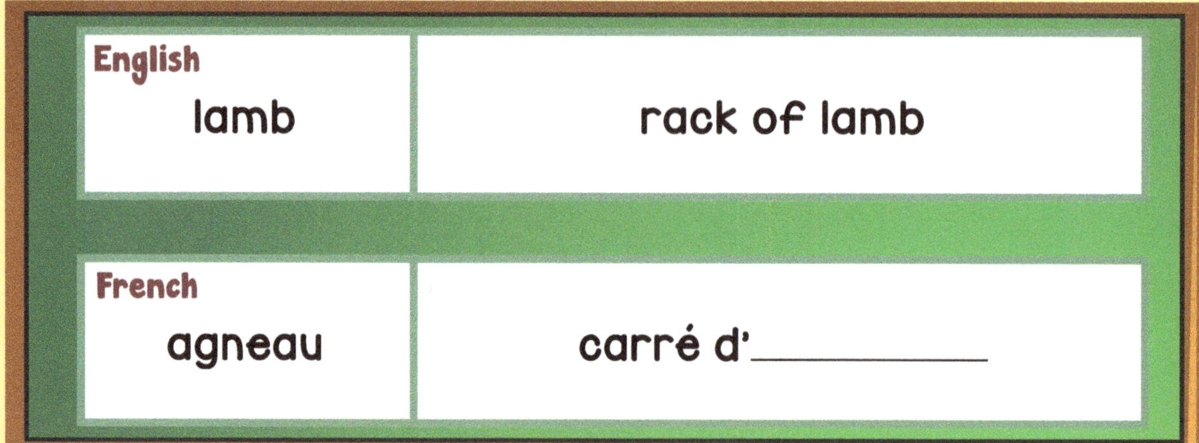

English	
lamb	rack of lamb

French	
agneau	carré d'____________

English	
fish	raw fish

French	
poisson	____________ cru

Fill in the blank with the correct French word.

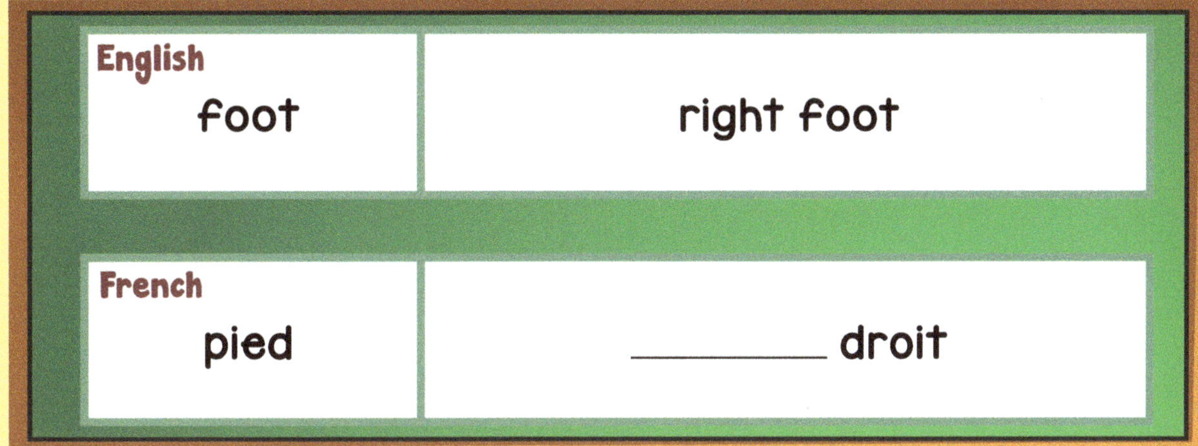

English	
foot	right foot

French	
pied	__________ droit

English	
leg	long legs

French	
jambe	longues __________s

Fill in the blank with the correct French word.

English	
head	head and neck

French	
tête	__________ et cou

English	
hand	left hand

French	
main	__________ gauche

Fill in the blank with the correct French word.

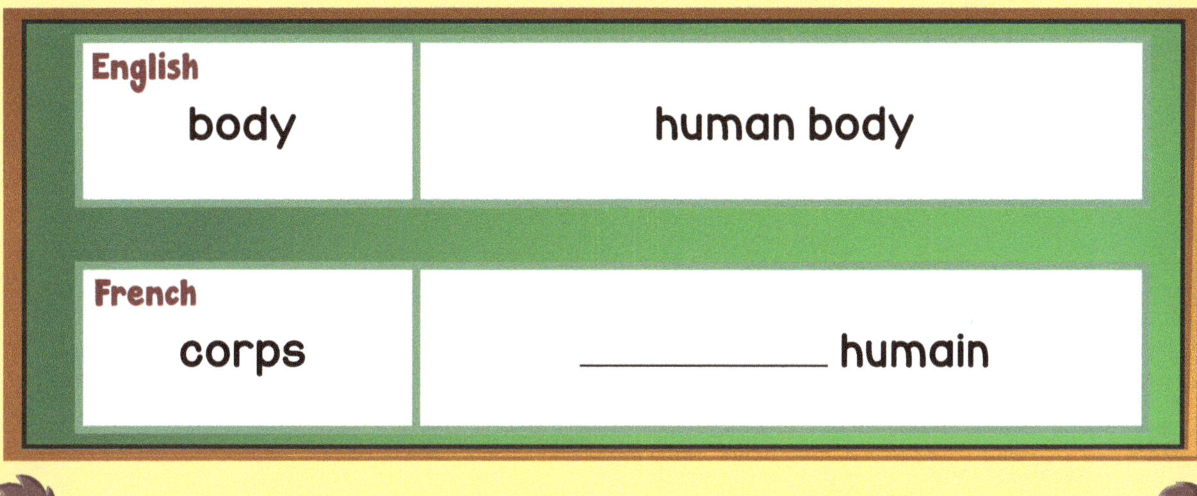

English	
body	human body

French	
corps	____________ humain

English	
stomach	model of a stomach

French	
estomac	maquette d'____________

Fill in the blank with the correct French word.

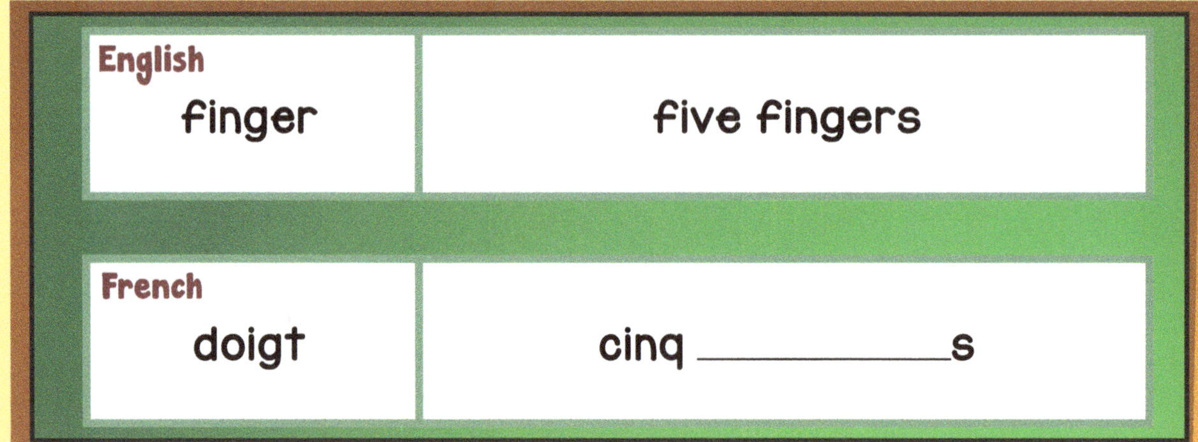

English	
finger	five fingers

French	
doigt	cinq ___________s

English	
arm	two arms

French	
bras	deux ___________

Here are some of the most common french phrases and expressions.

English

My name is...

French

Je m'appelle...

English

What is your name?

French

Comment vous appelezvous?

English
I don't understand.
French
Je ne comprends pas.

English
Thank you.
French
Merci.

English

You' re welcome.

French

De rien.

English

Excuse me.

French

Excusez-moi.

English

I love you.

French

Je t'aime.

English

I want to be with you.

French

Je veux être avec toi.

English

How are you?

French

Comment allez-vous?

English

It's okay.

French

Ça va.

English
Don't worry.
French
Ne vous en faites pas.

English
I don't understand.
French
Je ne comprends pas.

English

Do you speak English?

French

Parlez-vous anglais?

English

No problem.

French

Ce n'est pas grave.

English

I'm fine.

French

Je vais bien.

English

Let's go!

French

Allons-y!

English

I'm sorry.

French

Je suis désolé.

English

I don't know.

French

Je ne sais pas.

ANSWER KEY

MATCHING EXERCISE

Draw a line to match the English word to its French word.

with   et
and   monde
me   bon
good   avec
yesterday   moi
world   bonjour
hello   argent
money   hier

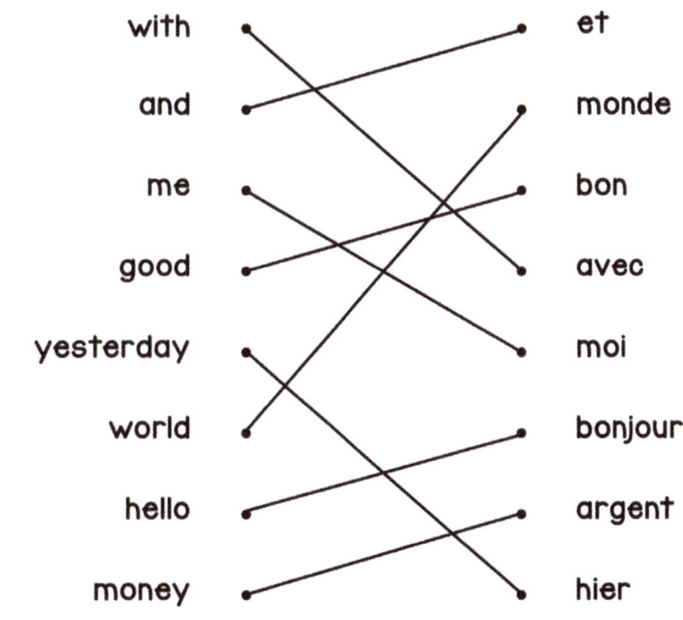

Visit
BABY PROFESSOR
EDUCATION KIDS
www.BabyProfessorBooks.com
to download Free Baby Professor eBooks and view
our catalog of new and exciting Children's Books